ZERO TO
INVESTED
IN LESS
THAN
60 MINUTES

Learn All The Tools To Becoming a Successful Investor in Less Than 60 Minutes

ACKNOWLEDGMENTS

I would like to thank my wife for inspiring me to start this project and for the support to allow me to follow through to its completion. Thank you to my family for being there for me.

DISCLAIMER:

This book is for informational purposes only, you should not construe any such information or other material as legal, tax, investment, financial, or other advice. Nothing contained in this book constitutes a solicitation, recommendation, endorsement, or offer by the author or any third-party service provider to buy or sell any securities or other financial instruments in any jurisdiction in which such solicitation or offer would be unlawful under the securities laws of such jurisdiction.

All content in this book is information of a general nature and does not address the circumstances of any particular individual or entity. Nothing in this book constitutes professional and/or financial advice, nor does any information in this book constitute a comprehensive or complete statement of the matters discussed or the law relating thereto. You alone assume the sole responsibility of evaluating the merits and risks associated with the use of any information or other content in this book before making any decisions based on such content. In exchange for using this book, you agree not to hold the author, its affiliates or any third party service provider liable for any possible claim for damages arising from any decision you make based on information or other content made available to you in this book.

CONTENTS

PREFACE

This book is a quick-to-consume, meat and potatoes book. I will guide you from knowing nothing about investing to being well on your way to reaching your wealth goals. My objective is to simplify the process to help you feel confident in starting your journey so you can watch your money and wealth grow over time.

Making your money work for you is one of the best ways to gain wealth. Compounding growth, even with small initial deposits, can do wonders over time. It is not just accumulating wealth, though; it is beating that ugly monster called inflation. Inflation is where the purchasing power of your dollar goes down. You can't find a candy bar for less than a dollar and those dollar menus no longer exist.

There used to be a time when opening a savings account would give you a decent return on your money and you may have had a chance that your deposits would grow and outpace inflation, but those times are gone. To find a place to park your cash—whether for retirement or just savings—and get respectable growth, exposure to the stock market is one of your best options.

ZERO TO MILLION, BABY!

Here is an example of how investing $500/MO over 30 years gets you to the MILLION mark.

		Results	
Starting Amount	$0		
After	30 years	**End Balance**	**$1,031,421.66**
Return Rate	10 %	Starting Amount	$0.00
Compound	annually	Total Contributions	$180,000.00
Additional Contribution	$500	Total Interest	$851,421.66

Contribute at the ◯ beginning ● end
of each ● month ◯ year

Calculate ▶

> You contributed (put-in) $180,000 over 30 yrs, but have a total of over $1.1 MILLION*

Balance Accumulation Graph

$1.5M

— Principal
— Interest
— Balance

$1.0M

$500.0K

$0

0yr 5yr 10yr 15yr 20yr 25yr 30yr

Breakdown

17%

83%

■ Total Contributions
■ Interest

Source; https://www.calculator.net/
* Based on 10% annual compound growth rate in the S&P 500 over the 30 years between 1992-2022

CHAPTER 1

WHY INVEST?
WHAT ARE STOCKS?

A lot of people may be intimidated when they hear "stocks" or "investing," especially if they were the sort to stick the money in a "guaranteed interest" savings account or stuff it under the proverbial mattress. But it doesn't have to be complicated. To keep it plain, stocks are literal shares of a company. You owning stock in a company is you owning a portion of the company. Why would a business do that, give away ownership, that is? What's in it for them? Well, at any given time, a company may need to raise money (capital). One way a business can raise capital is by "going public" and starting to sell shares in that company. You give the company money, and they give you a percentage of their company in return, and now you are an investor.

Okay, so here's where we learn how to make money from owning shares in the stock market. We know what a stock is, but what's the market part?

The market simply means the supply and demand for stocks in companies. On Day 1, also called the initial public offering (IPO), your share is worth what people are willing to pay for it. The idea is that the company that sold the stock will continue to grow and become more valuable. If the company continues to grow, then the price people are willing to pay for a share goes up. On the flip side, if a company fails to perform, then the price people are willing to pay for a share goes down. Basic supply and demand.

Now, you may be saying, "Dominic, I get that, but how do you pick the winners, the stocks that will go up!" That'll come soon, but for now, I just want to go over the basics. If you're following everything so far, great! If it is still a little unclear just remember that the more value people place on something, the higher the price (usually); and the opposite is also true when less value is placed on something. Got that part? Good! Let's move on.

CHAPTER 2

THE BIG PICTURE

In the last chapter, we found out that the "place" where stocks are bought and sold is called the stock market. It might help to think of the various markets as oceans. Within those oceans, there are different groups of stocks, like schools of fish. In the U.S. ocean are the domestic stocks, and the other oceans are the international stocks. The country's stocks are often used as representations of the economic activity of a given country.

Generally, stocks can be organized by company size, industry, growth perspectives, and relative value. But it's not actually that complicated. The good thing about organizing stocks is that some funds and indexes do the organizing for you. What do these funds and indexes do for you exactly? Well, they will pool these organized stocks into one investment group (or tool) for you. Some are a very specific mix of stocks chosen by a fund manager (an actual person who chooses stocks for you and your goals) and others are a group of a certain type of stock. These "preset groups" do not require a money manager as no particular stocks are being picked since the group is already there and categorized.

Let's say, for example, you want an upgrade on the clothes you have in your closet. Hypothetically, you can hire a designer and they can make you a customized wardrobe. This scenario takes time, effort, money, and skill. Hopefully, you hired a great designer who can fit your taste and knows how to dress you. If they can sense your style and your goals and they're great at what they do, you will get great value from buying a custom wardrobe. A second

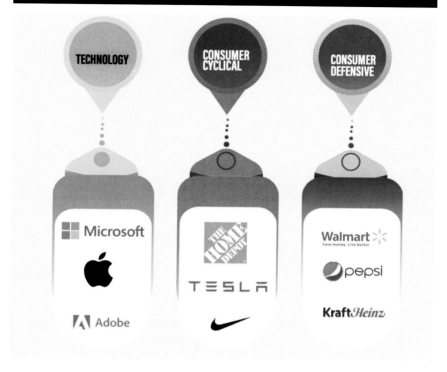

scenario is you fill your closet with a certain style of clothes, like suits. In this scenario, the clothes are either suits or they are not. Hiring a designer would be like investing in a fund that is run by a fund manager: You can get a great payoff but you have to find the right one and that can be difficult. Investing in a preset group would be more like the second scenario: Adding more suits to your closet might not make you the talk of the town but it will still upgrade your wardrobe.

For this explanation, we chose suits, but there are other groups as well, like jeans or hats. That's how index funds, or exchange-traded funds (ETFs) work. Instead of getting a mix of hand-picked items (stocks) chosen by the manager, we are just going to use an already organized group that we believe will grow in value over time.

Now, which fund is right for you will depend on your goals and, really, your knowledge. This book is focused on getting you in the investment game, keeping it simple, and getting you a return (making more money than you put in) on your investment. That being said, we will focus on what I consider the granddaddy of indexes, the S&P 500.

The S&P 500 is like someone recruiting the biggest and best 500 companies based in the United States and creating a super-team. In that team of 500 companies, you have different industries, the most recognizable names in the world like Apple, Google (now Alphabet), and Facebook (now Meta) among others. This is a simple, cookie-cutter way to bet on the U.S. economy.

When the economy is doing well, the stock market is usually doing well (going up in value) and the same is true on the other side, a bad economy means a bad market (going down in value). You've probably already experienced both. During the good times, you may remember people having jobs and satisfactory incomes, maybe some even made money by investing. During the bad times, it may have been hard to find work and make ends meet.

Oh, but what about investing during bad times, you say? There's always that story about somebody losing "damn near everything" they put in the market, or you may have lost money yourself. "Yeah, Dom, talk about that!" No problem.

CHAPTER 3

INFLATION: A MILE HANDICAP IN A MARATHON

This chapter goes out to my brown paper bag folks, the money under the mattress crew who do not trust anybody with their money. I get it, and I respect it. If you keep your cash with you, you know where it is and what it is doing; and that is the issue, it is doing nothing in that paper bag. If you do not have your money working for you, it is actually worse than nothing because you're losing value to that thief in the night called inflation. Inflation is the reason why just holding cash is "hustling backward" and while you may feel comfortable knowing that your cash is literally under your ass (or even in a savings account with 0.0001% annual interest), you are losing in the end.

What is inflation exactly? Let's get into that.

My definition of inflation is the value of your dollar going down, meaning that what you used to be able to buy with X amount of dollars, now costs more than X amount of dollars. In the famous words of Fat Joe, "Yesterday's price is not today's price!" That money in your pocket is in a constant race against inflation. The intensity of the race is not consistent: sometimes inflation runs slower, sometimes faster, but for the most part, it is running against the value of your money. So how fast is it running against your cash now? The Consumer Price Index (CPI) is usually the benchmark for measuring inflation. Although it's not perfect, it bundles up goods that we typically buy (like food, transportation, and medical care) and measures the cost of those goods over a period of time. As this book is being written in November 2022, the CPI percentage change from November 2021 to November 2022 is over 7%. The percentage change for energy is over 13%. Let's see any bank account give you a 5% annual return to keep up with the cost of food, let alone the 13% return needed to keep up with energy costs! Listen, you're sure as hell not keeping up with those numbers by stashing cash in a brown paper bag. The last few years, as we all know, have been exceptional, and since 2020 when COVID-19 caused a global pandemic, so many variables have been skewed. However, my point is: Your money is constantly facing headwinds, so you have to fight back to push ahead.

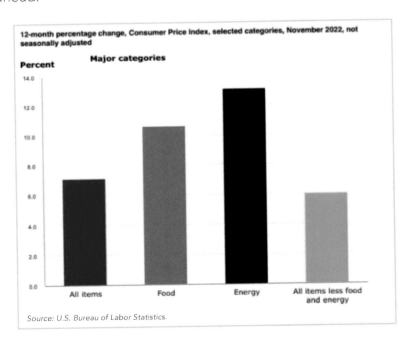

Source: U.S. Bureau of Labor Statistics.

Let's look at a longer time frame since we have had such strange years from 2020–2022. The 12-month percentage change over the last 20 years is shown above. What does this mean for you? Over the last 20 years, the value of the dollar has almost always gone down. Other than from February 2009 to October 2009, and a few months in 2015, inflation has been more than zero percent and has eaten away at your money. And when you're starting the marathon with a mile handicap, you will need some serious tools that can help you even the odds.

Note: Shaded area represents recession, as determined by the National Bureau of Economic Research.
Source: U.S. Bureau of Labor Statistics.

All right, so, where are we now? The buying power of your money goes down while your wages from your job stay about the same right? Right? Right.

I hear you saying: Dom, but that stock market stuff is risky. I know someone who lost nearly everything in the Recession. I appreciate that concern, so let's get into it.

CHAPTER 4

STOCKS AND INVESTING IS RISKY BUSINESS

One stock share of a company can go up in price or it can go down in price. If you bought a share and the price of that share goes up and you sell the share, then you made some gains (minus taxes and any expenses). On the flip side, if you bought a share and the price of that stock goes down and you sell the share, you have a loss on that stock. Until you close the transaction, meaning you sell the stock, those gains or losses are "unrealized." For example, you buying stock in George's A1 Peanut Butter (not an actual stock by the way . . . at least I don't think) will be "opening the position," the first half of a transaction. After you buy the stock, the price will fluctuate, and you will see your account balance reflect those changes. These changes in what the stock is worth, while you are still holding the stock are unrealized. Once you sell your shares of George's A1 Peanut Butter, then the gains or losses you made become "realized" and you make or lose money on those shares.

Once your gains or losses become realized, then you will either have more money than what you invested, break even, have less money than what you invested, or hypothetically, lose 100% of your capital (another term for the money you invested). These are the cold, hard facts that you have to know when you invest. Get rich quick or lose everything you invested are extremes and rare. In life, there are a lot of unknowns, but we do what we have to do every day despite the risks. Stepping outside your front door has some risks but you can be calculated about the risks and move with confidence.

All right, so you might be saying that this isn't too encouraging, Dom. You're supposed to be helping me start investing, not making me afraid to take the first step!

Look, that's the rare, worst-case scenario, so now let's talk about how you can keep investing and building wealth. It is all about keeping it simple, betting that the best economy in the world (the U.S. economy for those who haven't been paying attention) will be around and will do well in your lifetime, and keeping consistent with a little discipline.

> **"Get rich quick or lose everything you invested are extremes and rare"**

FlyByNightCompany.com
UP
1000%
A Week Ago...
IT WAS ALL
GOOD
JUST A
WEEK AGO.
BANK
RUPT
NOW...
FlyByNightCompany.com

CHAPTER 5

ON THE GOOD SIDE OF THE ODDS: INVESTING MADE SIMPLE

In the last chapter we went over the scary part . . . stocks can and often do go down in value. Now, here's the other truth: the stock market, over time, appreciates in value. What if I told you instead of trying to pick "winners" and doing stock analysis that even the most seasoned, professional investors have trouble with, you can just invest in the best companies in the United States in an all-in-one investment tool? Good, thought you would.

The S&P 500 is the all-in-one tool that can be your way to invest, save for retirement, and help outpace inflation. Let's touch on what exactly it is. Well, the Standard & Poors, the S and the P in S&P 500, is a credit rating company that has been around for over 100 years. Along with giving credit ratings to businesses, it is also known for creating indexes. In investing, an index is a way to group investments together (not necessarily stocks), into one investment vehicle, or product.

The S&P 500 is the group of 500 stocks that Standard & Poors believes are the best publicly traded companies in the United States. When most people are gauging the health of the stock market, this is probably the most used benchmark. Your favorite well-known companies like Apple, Microsoft, and Google are included in the S&P 500. So, what you're doing when you invest in it is betting on the best companies in the United States doing well over a period of time. The longer the period is, the higher the probability of your investment gaining in value.

Let's look at some historical facts, for all you numbers people out there. . Over 10 years, from November 2011 to November 2021, the annualized return (return on your investment over a year) is about 14.373%. Try making anything even close to 5% at a bank—not happening. Starting with a $1000 initial investment and adding just $100 a month can make a big difference in your life. It could make you a millionaire if you start early enough in your career and remain consistent.

There are years when the S&P has a negative return. During those down years, as counterintuitive as it may seem, you should invest more (buy low, sell high; we'll talk more about this in Chapter 8). Here is everything in a nutshell though. When you invest in the S&P, you are investing in some of the best and largest companies in the United States and over the long term, history shows you will make a return on what you have invested. That return has outpaced the rate of inflation and what your money can earn sitting in a conventional bank account.

Hopefully, now you're convinced that you do not want to be stuck on the sidelines when it comes to investing. You want to be in the game of wealth creation and money appreciation. The question is, where to start? You have a few options. In the next chapter, we will go over the options that may fit your situation.

CHAPTER 6

OPEN A RETIREMENT ACCOUNT

Outstanding! You have made your decision to make your money work for you and your family! You deserve a pat on the back. Now let's keep it moving and look at opening an account where you can start investing.

First, which of you have a 401(k) plan or a retirement plan through your employer? If you raised your hand, you need to take full advantage of that opportunity. Uncle Sam is giving you legal ways to save on a large amount of taxes that would have eaten at your gains. These types of accounts are meant for retirement. By you taking initiative in saving for retirement, the tax man gives you certain tax advantages. I am not a tax professional, so it would be smart to review with your tax advisor how these programs could be beneficial to you. Also, the rules and the contribution limits (how much money you can invest for the year) for these programs change often. It is good to do some homework for the current year's rule changes on the IRS website. Here are a few examples of employer-sponsored (meaning your job offers them) programs that may be available to you.

401(k)

A 401(k) is a retirement plan through your employer. Traditionally, you contribute money to the plan with dollars that have not been taxed, usually taken right out of your gross pay (your pay before any taxes or deductions). That money is then invested and any growth on the money is not taxed until you withdraw the funds.

The catch is that a 401(k) is meant for retirement, and what age does the IRS (currently) consider retirement age for your 401(k)? 59 and a half. What does that mean for you? If you withdraw money from your 401(k) before you are age 59 and a half, you will be taxed on that income and assessed a 10% penalty. There are some exceptions to the penalty, but again, I am not a tax professional, and if you are considering exercising any of the exceptions, you should contact your accountant. Regardless, you should start investing in a 401(k) with the mindset that this is a long-term retirement account.

IF YOU NEED HELP...

READ

Retirement Plan Document

CALL

Retirement Customer Service

TALK TO

Human Resources or Retirement Plan Advisors

403(b)

A 403(b) is similar to a 401(k) but this type of retirement vehicle is for nonprofit organizations and for government employees.

IRA

What if your employer does not have a retirement plan or you do not have traditional employment, but you still want to find a retirement vehicle that will give you tax benefits? There are two types of IRA and both give you tax advantages. A traditional IRA allows you to defer, or put off, paying taxes until you withdraw money from the account. A Roth IRA lets you use money that was already taxed (e.g., the money you have left after taxes and deductions were taken out of your paycheck) to contribute to your Roth IRA. The benefit here is that since your contributions were already taxed when they went in, the investment gains interest without being taxed when you withdraw. There are advantages to both traditional and Roth IRAs. If you decide to open an IRA, you can consult an advisor or tax professional to find the best fit for your situation and goals.

The IRS website is a great tool to review retirement planning and the details of each type of program. Check it out at www.irs.gov.

LOG IN

CHAPTER 7

OPEN A BROKERAGE ACCOUNT

We looked at retirement funds through your employer, so next we look at the brokerage account. Today, it's easy to open an account with any number of brokers—TD Ameritrade, Fidelity, Robinhood, etc. There is no right or wrong answer to which brokerage account works best for you, however, you will want to look at fee structures, such as commissions for trading.

YouTube is a great resource for looking at the interface or the layout of the brokerage platform. What we are talking about in this book has set and forget strategy for long-term wealth building. Whichever company you choose, try to feel comfortable with the platform and research their fees. The good thing about brokerage firms these days is that they usually have low fees and zero commissions.

Do the research and find which brokerage platform is comfortable for you.

SCAN FOR RESOURCES

CHAPTER 8

INVESTING IN A S&P 500 FUND

Here are some basics of exchange-traded funds (ETFs) and index funds when it comes to investing in the S&P 500. ETFs and index funds are designed to get the same or similar performance as the index it follows. Usually, in mutual funds, a fund manager picks the investments for the fund, but in an index fund, the investments are already selected because it is just following the index, e.g., the S&P 500 or the Dow Jones. What does that mean for you?

First, it means simpler investing. Again, investing in the benchmark index, the S&P, gives you one of the closest things to a set-and-forget investment style you can have. Compared to other mutual funds, ETFs and index funds are usually cheaper. Why? Fund managers don't have to do the stock picking; the stocks and investments are already picked for them, and all they have to do is follow the index. Many mutual funds require a fund manager to choose the investments and they need to get paid for their efforts. Who pays? The investor (you), and most funds do not outperform the S&P 500 in the long run.[1] Vanguard and Fidelity are two good names in the index and ETF space. Once you choose the S&P fund from your preferred company (for example, the Vanguard S&P 500 ETF, symbol VOO, or the Fidelity 500 Index Fund, symbol FXAIX) you can decide your method of making contributions (adding to the money invested).

[1] Aly J. Yale, "Index funds vs. Mutual funds: What's the difference?," Business Insider, July 7, 2022, https://www.businessinsider.com/personal-finance/index-fund-vs-mutual-fund

The easiest way to keep investing regularly is called dollar cost averaging (DCA). DCA is simply investing the same amount of money at the same interval. For example, let's say you are paid every two weeks, you can contribute a certain dollar amount, maybe $100 every two weeks, into your S&P 500 fund. You can set this up to be done automatically through your brokerage account. No worries. Just check your account every few months or so. When you get a raise, increase your contributions. Congratulations on giving your future self a pay raise.

The second method takes more attention and discipline. You will still have to be consistent with contributions, but when the market is low, you will add greater amounts to your ETF/index fund investment. How can you tell when the market is low? I will go over a couple of ways that really do not take much time or effort to monitor.

> **"If you believe in that investment, then when the price is down, you should buy more of it because you get more bang for your buck."**

If you see it in the news

Not just any news, I am talking about non-investment-related news. Business news talks about the stock market all the time, but when you start hearing about how bad the market is all the time from non-business news sources it is probably a good time to start buying. Hearing stories on the radio or your local news (again, not the business part) is a good indicator. Once stock market happenings make it to regular news media, it's generally a good time to start plowing extra dollars into the market. Think about it, your local music radio station and your evening news will cover almost anything else before they look at the stock market, so when they do cover it, it is most likely negative news. Those are the times to play it smart and buy into your fund at a "sale" price.

200-day moving average

If you want to see how your investment is doing over the long term, then pay attention to its 200-day moving average. Keeping with the theme of the book, let's use the simple moving average (SMA), which is a series of points on a chart that make a line that follows the average closing price of the last 200 market sessions. This line is your 200-day SMA. If the price of your investment is below the 200-day SMA line, that means the price is relatively low compared to where the investment has been historically—over the last 200 days—and it may be time to increase how much money you are investing.

If you believe in that investment, then when the price is down, you should buy more of it because you get more bang for your buck. In the case of the S&P 500, you are basically betting on some of the best companies in the

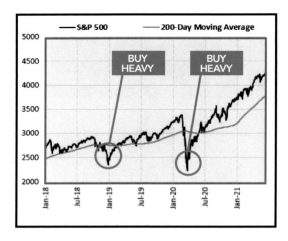

U.S., very similar to betting on the U.S.A. as a whole. The odds are in your favor with this, folks. There are plenty of tools out there on how to set up a 200-day moving average for the brokerage account you chose. You can look at the YouTube channels of your chosen account provider (refer to the Resources section). If all else fails, call your fund's customer service and they may be able to guide you through the process.

Listen to people and do the opposite

If working with charts or watching the news is not your thing, then there is another easy option. Listen out for people who complain about their accounts going down in value. Even better, if those same people were showing off about their balance when the market did well. Even better than that, if they were talking about trading when the money was easy to make and now they shut up or are calling the market a scam, it is time to go in heavy! These are all indications the market is falling and that it's time to up your investments.

CHAPTER 9

GETTING YOUR MONEY

The hardest part about investing is starting the process, but even that's getting easier every day. More brokerage firms are in business, which means more competition and better options for the consumer. Opening an account now and organizing your settings and investments is not much harder than registering a social media account and learning the features. I'm glad you made it this far with me because now you are on your way to creating some real value for yourself and your loved ones.

OK, Dom, but when can I actually get my money? Technically, anytime you want*, but hopefully you will have the discipline to let the money accumulate, grow, and compound so you can have at least a nice supplement to your spending for when you'll need the cash . . . like at retirement. If you are lucky enough to have a 401(k) or another similar employer-sponsored retirement plan, invest in that! It gives you tax advantages while you are accumulating. Yet, there are penalties if you make a withdrawal before you reach retirement age. (Retirement age is determined by the IRS, and at the time of writing, retirement age is 59 and a half years old.) If you decide to withdraw funds out of a 401(k), or another tax-deferred account, before retirement age, you may be assessed penalties associated with taking money out of the account before the IRS retirement age.

Withdrawals on a regular, brokerage account (meaning there is no special tax treatment for that account) are taxed as capital

* Review your organization's retirement plan rules. There may be additional restrictions on the ways you can access funds from your employer-sponsored retirement account.

gains. That means whatever portion of your transaction is a profit, that amount will be taxed at whatever the rate for capital gains is at that time. You can check what the federal capital gains tax is on irs.gov. Consulting a tax professional can help you plan, too.

In general, it is ideal to start young and let your money grow over 30+ years of employment. Consistent DCA over time and giving yourself a pay raise by increasing contributions can create amazing results. The S&P 500 has an annual return of about 10%. I'm sure you would love to see that 10% return on $500,000 and upwards, so keep at it and let your money do the work for you.

CONCLUSION
Getting Your Money

There, you made it. You're an investor. While this is not meant to be an all-inclusive guide for everything to do with investing, you read the book and followed the simple steps—you are on your way to building wealth and security for yourself and your family.

RESOURCES

Zero To Invested YouTube

www.youtube.com/@ZeroToInvested

Fidelity YouTube

www.youtube.com/@Fidelity

The "Investing for Beginners" section goes over topics and questions for new investors

TD Ameritrade YouTube

www.youtube.com/@TDAmeritrade

Great educational videos in the investing basics

Robinhood YouTube

www.youtube.com/@RobinhoodApp

Great "How To" section.

Investopedia

www.investopedia.com

www.youtube.com/@Investopedia

For learning about financial terms and concepts, from beginner to advanced

IRS Retirement Plans Page

www.irs.gov/retirement-plans

Keep up with contribution limits and tax rules for your retirement plans

SEC's Investors Education Page

www.investor.gov

Useful stuff like the Compound Interest Calculator in the "Financial Tools & Calculators" section helps you plan your investment goals

Your Human Resources, Retirement Plan Customer Service and Plan Documents

If you have a retirement plan through your employer, take the time to review the plan rules or talk to an advisor or customer service representative familiar with the plan. Your Human Resources department will be able to give guidance on what help is available.

NOTES

DEFINITIONS

200 Day Simple Moving Average (SMA) – The average price of the last 200 days performance of an asset, plotted out on a chart

401(k) – A retirement plan through your employer that gets special tax treatment by the IRS

403(b) – A retirement plan through your non-profit employer that gets special tax treatment by the IRS

Broker – Individual or entity that buys and sells assets on your behalf

Brokerage Account – An investment account opened with a brokerage company. Not a retirement account where the IRS gives special tax treatments and rules regarding contributions and withdrawals

Capital Gains – The earnings made from an investment before taxes

Compounding Growth – Where an asset's earnings are reinvested to generate additional returns

Consumer Price Index (CPI) – A measure that tracks the price of goods and services

Contribution Limit – The maximum amount you can contribute to your retirement plan

Dollar Cost Averaging (DCA) – Contributing the same dollar amount to your investment with consistent frequency

Domestic Stocks – Stocks that are located in the country you live in

Employer-Sponsored Plan – A retirement plan through your employer

Exchange Traded Fund (ETF) – A fund traded on a stock exchange that usually tracks the performance of an index or asset

Indicator – A tool used to help predict the direction or climate of a financial asset or the stock market

Individual Retirement Account (IRA) – A retirement plan, not associated with an employer, that an individual can open and contribute to, that gets special tax treatment by the IRS

Inflation – an increase in prices and decrease in the value of money

Return – is the money made or lost on an investment over a period of time

Index Fund – A portfolio of stocks and bonds made to copy the make-up and performance of a financial index

International Stocks – Stocks that are located in a foreign country

Mutual Fund – A pooled investment where many investors contribute to the fund and the money is invested in stocks, bonds, etc

Recession – A downturn in the economy for an extended period of time

S&P 500 – An index of the 500 largest publicly listed companies in the United States

Stock Market – Where buyers and sellers meet to purchase and sell shares of public companies

Supply and Demand – The amount of goods and services available in comparison to the amount of goods and services consumers want to buy

Unrealized Gain/Loss – The gain or loss from an investment that has not been locked in because the investment has not been sold

Withdrawal – Taking money from an investment account, usually referring to a retirement account, such as a 401(k)

Made in the USA
Middletown, DE
14 August 2023

36362550R00022